Chapter One

My name is Malachi, but everybody calls me Toothpick. I am a cedar tree and also I live in the Woodland of the Giant Trees. My dad, Obadiah, and also my grandpa, Hezekiah, were both cedar trees in the woodland as well, and they still are very important trees in the history of our land.

below the mountainsides.
I call him Uncle Woody, yet his actual name is Ashkenaz. He has been made into the top of the king's seminar table. All the consultants to the king sit around Uncle Woody as well as make all the important decisions of the kingdom.
And afterwards there is my dad-- Obadiah. He was the king of this woodland before the imperial lumberjacks reduced him down and also took him for an extremely special function.
Numerous carpenters were selected by the king himself to make my daddy into the door of the throne area. When the king or queen give their permission, my dad shields the king and is just opened up. He is a thick door and he is ten feet high and he evaluates numerous hundred pounds.
Knowledgeable artists have actually painted three eagles on my father's thick wood as well as polished him to ensure that he beams virtually like glass.
With all those magnificent family members, you would believe that the remainder of the trees in the forest would treat me special, as well.

However, that is not the instance. Most of the trees laugh at me. I am still young-- only regarding 15 rings old-- however even so, I am brief for my age. Except for the twin willow trees (Moggy and also Foggy), I am the fastest tree regarding I can see. I am so tiny that most of the trees call me Toothpick. I do not like the name quite due to the fact that I think I am still large enough to be made right into something unique for someone.

When the woodsmen come into the Forest of the Titan Trees, all the trees stand tall and large, so the woodsmen will pick them. And also when I stand high and also big, the woodsmen don't appear to discover me, as well as they continue strolling.

Each time they choose among the bigger trees, the remainder of the trees laugh as well as point their branches at me calling, "Toothpick, Toothpick--never ever the one they choose. Toothpick, Toothpick, he is also small also for a home for wooden dolls. Which's the tooth."

When David and his calf got in the forest ...

Chapter Two

" Oh, hi. I didn't see you there. My name is David. Thanks for reading my tale. This is my papa's barn. I just turned ten years old as well as my papa provided me a wonderful present for my birthday-- a young calf bone. We have several cows and my dad increases them and feeds them as well as provides water to consume alcohol. Among my chores is to clean up the barn on a daily basis and also make sure that the cows are not ill. However I have actually never ever possessed a cow all my very own. I simply aid my daddy look after his cows.

Last week my dad offered me with my initial cow to raise all by myself. I

hope this calf bone will certainly be my friend.
A calf bone, a calf, this newborn calf bone is mine. I'll feed him, as well as I'll care for him,.
I'm so satisfied today.
Yes, I'm absolutely happy today. Blue skies are coming my method and also every little thing's mosting likely to be alright. I'm the proprietor of a newborn calf bone.
Currently what a lot more can I say, Hey, Hey, Hey, Hey, Hey.".
" Let me present you to my calf. Wait a minute ... I have actually not chosen a name yet. As you can see, he is a white cow with brown places. Allow's see how he reacts to some of my favorite ideas. I know it needs to be a special name and also I hope he will agree when he hears it.".

" Okay cow, what do you think about Ithamar?" The cow trembled his head and also sneezed.
" Not so good, uh? I such as Peter Pumpernickel! How about that name?" The cow mooed like he was injured as well as ready to regurgitate.
" No? Do not shed your lunch over it. Let's attempt Belshazzar.".
The calf transformed his face away from David as well as stared at the wall.
" Okay, an additional negative option. How about Jerubabble, Shinbone, or Mickmash?".
The cow in fact surrendered on his back as well as kicked his back legs in denial.
" Jumping Jehoshaphat, cow! I give up.".
The cow stood up as well as began to moo excitedly.

" What did I state? What was it?".

The cow remained to moo and also nodded his head.
" What is going on? Jumping Jehoshaphat, calm down.".

The cow relocated close to David as well as scrubed his head versus his tee shirt.
" Oh, I obtain it. Let me introduce you to my new calf bone, Jumping Jehoshaphat." The cow shook his head in agreement.
" How regarding I call you J.J. for short?" The calf jumped up and down with delight.
" Excuse me for a minute. Right here comes my father.".
" Daddy, let me introduce you to Leaping Jehoshaphat, yet I am going to call him J.J.".

David's daddy looked into the cow's big brown eyes. What a great name. This calls for a celebration.

As he put the bell around the calf's neck he claimed, "Now David can hear you coming and also recognize where you are when he desires you. I assume you have whatever you need except for one point.".
Jehoshaphat mooed, as well as David asked, "What else does he need, Dad?".
David's dad stated and smiled, "J.J. has actually been attempting to consume with the remainder of the cows and they are not sharing their food really well. He has actually just been getting the leftovers as well as have to wait for the older cows to obtain done before he can enjoy any kind of food in all. I think he needs his own feed trough. Every pet needs his own dish and your calf requires his own area to consume.

What do you state? Let's enter into the forest, choose a wonderful tree, sufficed down, and also I will make it into an unique feed trough for Jehoshaphat.".

" Wow, yes, that seems good. May I pick the tree? Can J.J. come, as well?".

" Certainly, you can choose the tree and of course, the calf can come along," stated David's father. "You prepare; I'll get my axe; as well as I'll satisfy you out in the front of the barn.".

I have to go and also find a tree simply right for Jehoshaphat. Wait, why don't you come along?

Chapter Three

Earlier in the early morning before the calf bone as well as the child arrived, the trees were waking up as the sunlight cast a gorgeous red as well as orange radiance on the eastern clouds. People can't hear trees chat, however if they could, they would have listened to the talk among the trees.

" Ahh, what a good evening's sleep. It looks like an additional attractive day in your area. Hey, Ralph, are you awake yet?".

" Oh yep, Sid," said Ralph. "The sun feels mighty excellent this morning. I simply need to stretch my trunk and branches a little as well as I'll prepare to stand tall and have a tree-mendous morning."

Sid laughed, "Don't extend your branches too much as well as create your fallen leaves to fall off. It's not even September yet as well as you seem to be dropping your leaves.

faster than common. Perhaps it suggests age.".
" You're not that old, Ralph," called Sophia, a gorgeous tree with flowing environment-friendly leaves. "But your trunk seems a little droopy-- perhaps you need much more workout.".
Ralph looked angry and replied to Sophia. "Well, a minimum of I don't color my roots.".
Sid giggled much more, "You individuals are so amusing. I can not quit giggling. Also my bark is drinking at your absurd jokes.".
Ralph trembled his branches and elevated his voice, 'Shhhhhh ... Pay attention, what is that sound?".

A high-pitched audio originated from amongst the trees.
Sid quietly giggled, "That is a snore. Toothpick is still reducing zzzz's.".
Ralph said, "No, it seems more like a frog with a pest caught in its throat.".
Sophia participated in, "No way, it's a yellow-bellied, log-nosed, purple-eyed, white-crested, three-toed dragonfly."

" Or perhaps it's a donkey that just ingested an onion," included Sid.

All 3 trees laughed so loud that Toothpick got up.
" What? Oh, good morning, people," stated Toothpick as he yawned and also stretched his little branches.
" Well," said Sid, "if it isn't the smallest family member-- scrawny little Toothpick.".
" Simply getting up, little cedar branch?" asked Sophia. "The sunlight's been up for hrs.".
" Do not badger him, Sophia," claimed Ralph. "He's so small - he doesn't obtain the sunlight's rays till midday.".
They all laughed and also drank their branches at him.
" Maybe I'm not the tallest tree, but I'll grow. I'll allow like you one day," claimed Toothpick.

Ralph's smile went away and also he practically whispered, "Do not count on it, Stubby. We are the kings and also queens of the woodland land.

Sid sneered, "Yeah, Toothpick. We are the tall giants as well as you are simply a shrimp.".

Sophia rolled her eyes, "I want you didn't have origins. We would certainly make you move to the various other side of the woodland due to the fact that if you really did not. You just don't belong here.".

Toothpick wished he didn't have roots either, so he can hide as well as run and also leave the forest behind.

The remainder of the trees were still laughing when Sid heard the sound.

Stand tall.

Ralph claimed, "Maybe it's the imperial woodsmen searching for a cedar to make into an upper body to hold all the king's prize.".

" Or a tall, straight tree to be the watercraft's pole to hold the sails so the king can cross the sea, sail worldwide, and check out the kings and also queens of other countries," added Sophia.

" Hey, Ralph, consider Toothpick. He's attempting to stand tall, too," buffooned Sid. "As if any person would desire him," laughed Ralph.
" Shhh!" hissed Sophia as all the trees silenced down waiting to see who was entering the woodland.

Chapter Four

" Wow, J.J., consider those trees. Aren't they high and also straight?! This is precisely what we require," said David as the child and his calf got to a beautiful part of the woodland.
Jehoshaphat mooed rather loudly and also shook his head.
" Daddy, come and look. I assume we have actually discovered the best trees," David called.
Waiting on his papa to find, David and also the calf checked out each tree meticulously. "One of these will make a terrific feed trough for you, J. J. All we need to do is.

find the best one.".

Sid whispered to Ralph so silently that David could not hear, "Hey, Ralph."

"What do you desire, Sid?".

" Did that little young boy say he desired one of us for a feed trough?".

" Yes, I assume he did. Can you photo living throughout the day in a hot barn and also holding food regularly for a smelly old calf?".

" That's not for me. I do not want anything to do with barns as well as foolish moo- moos.".

Toothpick just smiled, "I think the little calf bone is kind of cute.".

Sophia rolled her eyes once more, "Toothpick, only you would assume a cow was cute.".

My daddy, Obadiah, as well as my grandfather, Hezekiah, were both cedar trees in the woodland as well, and also they still are very crucial trees in the background of our land. Other than for the twin willow trees (Moggy and also Foggy), I am the quickest tree as far as I can see. Every time they pick one of the larger trees, the remainder of the trees laugh and point their branches at me calling, "Toothpick, Toothpick-- never the one they pick. Earlier in the morning prior to the calf bone and also the kid arrived, the trees were waking up as the sun cast an attractive red as well as orange radiance on the eastern clouds. People can't listen to trees talk, yet if they could, they would certainly have heard the talk among the trees.

Sid checked out the other trees and also stated, "I don't find out about the remainder of you people, yet I am going to look as puny and sick as I can and just hope that the little child passes me on by."

" You understand it, Sid. I'm beginning to feel weak already."

" My branches hurt." "I'm feeling faint; the sun is as well hot," came the whispers of the other trees. Toothpick continued to stand as tall as possible.

As David's papa caught up with his kid, David turned and said, "Papa, J.J. and I discovered some terrific looking trees! Come and also look. What do you think?"

David's daddy looked as well as stopped up at the high trees. "Oh, yes. Among these trees will do quite nicely. If we select a big one, I will have adequate timber to replace my workbench and maybe even make a rake for the areas."

" And also you claimed that I could choose it out?" asked David.
"Take your choice. Look them over and discover the best one."
David and J. J. strolled down the line of trees, quit at numerous, and tried to decide which one was ideal. They stopped at Sid and saw just how high the tree was. The child and calf bone considered each various other, shook their heads "no," and continued to look.

When they concerned Toothpick, J.J. quit and smelled Toothpick's trunk. David examined his branches. The child and also calf bone turned towards each other and appeared to concur that this would certainly be their choice.
" Father, this is the one This is the tree we desire," claimed David with enjoyment.
David's papa came over to evaluate the tree. He looked dissatisfied.
" Oh, that's a good, high tree, Dad, but there's truly something about this one.

"I believe it will do.
The calf bone started to dance around, and David clapped his hands.

" Alright after that, this set it will be!" responded David's papa as he lowered the delighted tree to take him residence.

As the kid, his daddy, and also the calf bone left taking Toothpick with them, the trees started to chatter once more,

" Wow, was that ever close. Picture, I was nearly a serving tray for a pet," said Sid.

" A feed trough, a plow, as well as a workbench. What a typical task for one of the excellent kings of the cedar trees," stated Ralph with an unfortunate voice.

Sid stated, "They will certainly be lucky if they obtain enough timber from Toothpick for the feed trough."

" I sort of pity Toothpick, the little electric razor," shared Sophia. "Simply to assume his father is the door of the throne room, and he is mosting likely to assist feed animals. What a waste."
Ralph just giggled, "Well, I, for one, rejoice to see him go."

Chapter Five

A couple of days after David as well as J.J. chose Toothpick from the forest, the young boy and his calf were playing a video game of tag in the barnyard. " Tag, you're it!" laughed David as he tapped Jehoshaphat on the shoulder.

David removed running in the opposite instructions and also the calf bone began to chase him. David ran in a zig-zag pattern, initially to the left, then to the right, after that directly ahead, before making a sharp turn back to the. As rapid as David ran, Jehoshaphat was simply too quick. David really felt the mild push of the

calf bone's nose on his back as well as saw J.J. zooming previous him like a race steed. Jehoshaphat jumped in the air and also allow out a loud moo. David fell down laughing as he saw just how much his calf bone was enjoying the chase. J.J. saw David drop and involved see if he was injured. David hid his face up until the calf bone was almost upon him. He leapt to his feet, touched the calf bone on his nose and also ran as quick as he could screaming, "Leaping Jehoshaphat, you're it again!"
Jehoshaphat quickly caught his master. David chuckled once again as well as claimed, "Okay, all right, you are as well fast for me. I quit. You win."
The calf came running over and also place his head to have his ears scratched.

David happily damaged Jehoshaphat's ears as he informed him how much he liked playing with him, "J.J., you are the best cow. We are terrific pals as well as I am so thankful that Papa provided you to me."

" Wait, do you listen to that?" David claimed. "Listen to that sound from the barn. If Marvel has dad has actually your new feed trough, i.

wonder. That was sawing, and also now I listen to the pounding of a hammer.".

Jehoshaphat turned his head from one side to the other, like a young puppy listening to weird audios. He made a soft moo and also his tail started to wag.

" Allow's go and also watch," stated David as he began to approach the barn. The calf followed and quickly they reached the barn door and also might see inside. David's papa was hard at job. He was hammering and whistling as he meticulously crafted the wood.

" That looks truly great, Daddy," said David.
His dad reversed, "Well, thanks, boy. Come as well as see the tree we chopped down. He doesn't resemble a tree now. I need to smooth down a couple of harsh edges. I desire to give the trough an attractive layer of green paint.
The paint will take a while to completely dry, however the trough needs to be ready tomorrow early morning ... just in time for morning meal.".
Jehoshaphat mooed his authorization and David slapped his hands.

Toothpick was very satisfied with his make over. David's daddy had utilized patience as well as real ability in making him strong as well as rugged. He felt helpful as well as might see the pleasure that he was giving David as well as J.J. What a change from the forest where the trees made fun of him and informed jokes concerning his dimension. He was enjoyed have buddies like David as well as Leaping Jehoshaphat-- a taken on family that would enjoy him and also care for him. He was also extremely ecstatic concerning getting a new layer. Eco-friendly was among his preferred colors.

Chapter Six

David, J.J., as well as Toothpick had so much fun with each other. Every morning David would certainly generate some food for the calf bone, put it in Toothpick's arms, and also the three of them would certainly chat as well as laugh together.

Occasionally David would certainly tell jokes and J.J. would laugh his insane moo. Toothpick would certainly laugh too, due to the fact that the jokes were funny and J.J.'s moo was also funnier.

David would state, "J.J. what do you call a cow that has consumed excessive?".

J.J. would just consider David awaiting the solution.
" A pig." All three would poke fun at the idea of a cow being a pig.
David took a look at J.J and asked, "J.J., why did we placed a bell around your neck?".
J.J. virtually went cross-eyed attempting to see his bell.
" Since your horns don't work." David said. J.J. laughed so much he fell over.
" As well as Toothpick, why did the woodsman inform you the exact same story 4 days straight?".
Toothpick glanced at J.J. as well as the calf trembled his head. David stated, "Since he knew you wood knot be board.".
David would certainly also inform jokes regarding himself. "Why did David ask the mailman to aid him to mean the word, hippopotamus?".
After a pause, he said, "Since the mailman was so great with letters.".
After they chuckled with each other until they were out of breath, the 3 sang and danced all over the barn. David would do a jig as J.J. stomped his feet as well as Toothpick hummed a woodchopper song. After that David would put

Toothpick on J.J.'s back so he might ride around the barn while David sang a track about a royal prince riding into the sundown.
Toothpick suched as the nights ideal of all. David would inform them of his desires of ending up being a male simply like his daddy.

" My dad is the best male I know," David would certainly state. "He provides food and also cash to those that have little. Every person in the town claims he is a great and also sincere male.
Someday, I will be just like him.".
Toothpick would certainly think of his father when David shared these points about his papa. Toothpick liked David and also J.J.

Chapter Seven

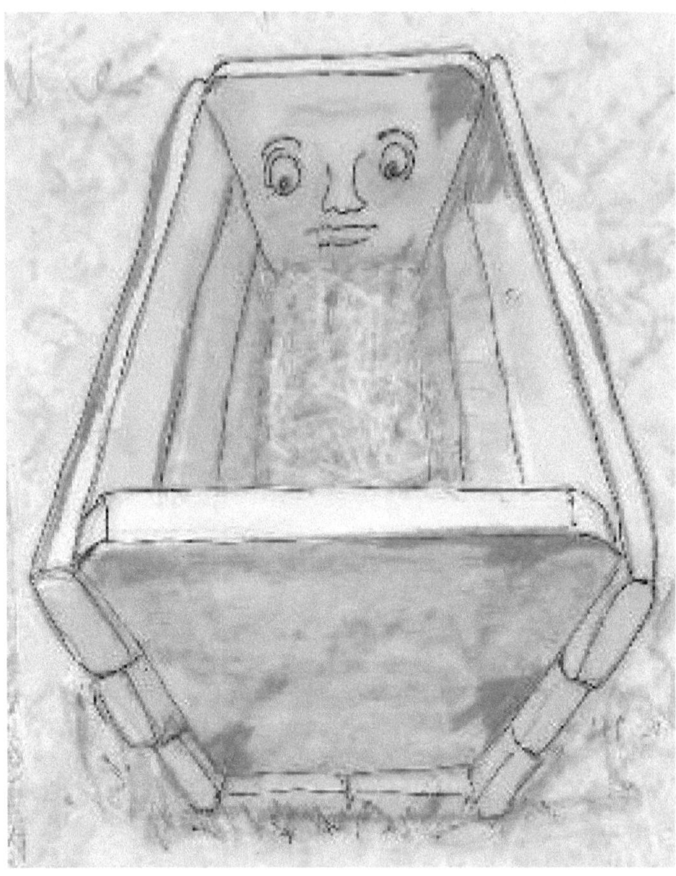

Hello there, it's me once more. You may not even identify me, but it's me, Toothpick. I have actually transformed quite a bit gradually. It's been many years given that David as well as J.J. discovered me in the Forest of the Giant Trees. The three of us invested lots of delighted days playing and also chuckling and speaking with each other. I was so happy to be with them. The

three people grew old together in this special barn.
Yet Jehoshaphat is currently a full-grown cow enjoying a lot of his days eating.

David is no longer a child however has actually taken over his daddy's organization. David is a crucial guy in the village now.
Although the barn is great and also cozy today, throughout the years, the rainfall and cold have made my boards warp. I utilized to obtain a new layer of paint each year. I have actually been yellow, red, brownish, as well as orange. As you can see, my paint is peeling, as well as I might desperately use a new coat to look my ideal.

I think the various other trees were right when they claimed I was too little to become anything worthwhile. In fact, I am not made use of for anything any longer, other than to hold some food for the pets of tourists staying at David's inn. It can be really unfortunate to seem like I benefit nothing. If only a person could utilize me for something.

What's that? Do you hear voices? I assume a person is coming. That may be David, however I hear a number of voices with him. I must be quiet currently, so I can hear their discussion.

I have never seen so many visitors coming into the city. I utilized to play in below with my calf, J.J., when I was a boy.".

" We will certainly be fine in here, sir," stated the male walking with David.
" Oh yes, thanks for your generosity, sir," came the words of a woman as her partner aided her down from the donkey's back.
" I desire I had something much better. This barn has not been used for quite some time," responded David.

“We understand,” said the man. “We’ve traveled a long distance today and a dry, soft place to lay our heads is greatly welcomed, especially since my wife is expecting our first child any day now.”

The woman smiled, and David nodded his head and said, “Then, I will let you get your rest. If I can do anything for you, please let me know.”

“Thank you. God bless you and good night,” whispered the young woman as she sat down on the hay.

“Good night to you both,” said David as he left the barn, closing the door behind him.

The man turned to his wife, “You must be exhausted, Mary. Rest while I get you some water to drink and some dried fruit. I’ll look after the donkey. It has been quite a day and a long journey.”

“Thank you, Joseph, but you must rest, too. You are a very good husband to find this place of safety for us.”

After some nourishment (that’s a big word for food and drink) the couple made a comfortable bed out of the hay and fell deeply asleep.

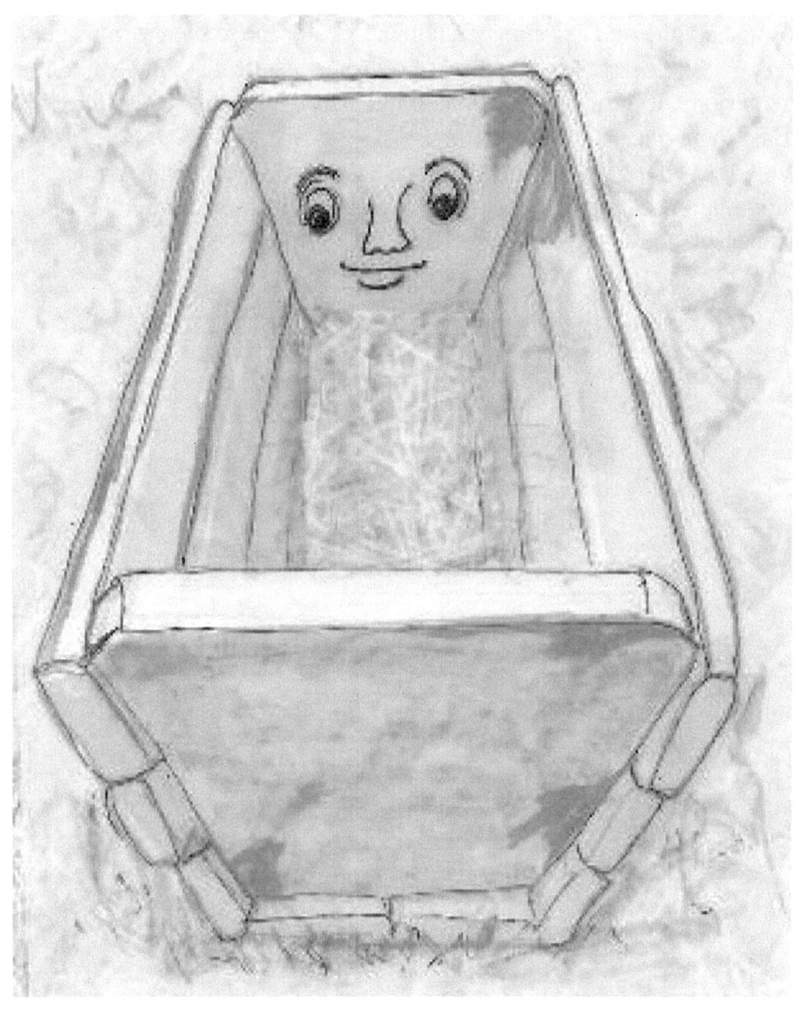

Hello, it's Toothpick. I'm back. Did you hear that? David's business is going so well that he is sold out this evening. He has always been kind to others and it looks like he is trying to provide for this man and his wife so that they don't have to sleep on the street tonight. They seemed grateful for the room.

Everything is nice and quiet out here in the barn. It is dark tonight, but fortunately the moon is shining enough light for me to see the young couple sleeping in the hay. There is a sense of peace in here that I have not felt for many years. It is quiet and calm and it makes me feel like everything is going to be fine.

Well, I'd better get some sleep, too, in case David or this young man and his wife might need me in the morning. I will let you know if anything special happens. Good-bye for now.

Chapter Eight

Psst! Hey, it's me again. Toothpick. I don't want to bother you, but something amazing happened last night, something truly amazing. A couple of hours after I went to sleep last night, I woke up when I heard the young man and his wife making some noise. I soon realized that it was time for the baby to be born. I got so excited because, as far as I know, a human baby had never been born in the barn before.

It was not too long after I woke up that I heard the cry of a baby. I also heard Mary crying for joy and Joseph laughing as they celebrated the birth of their first-born child. It was a boy.

I heard Joseph say, "Mary, we have a son. You have given birth to a boy." Mary replied, "Yes, my husband, and we shall call him Jesus!"

Joseph hugged them both and then he lifted his son toward the sky and thanked God for the blessing of their son. Joseph also thanked God for His provision of a place for his son's birth. He gave the child back to his wife and took some soft, clean hay and placed it in my arms. Joseph turned back to the baby, wrapped him in clean strips of cloth, and then, you won't believe what he did. He laid the child in my arms.

I felt strangely important. It was such an honor to hold a child who was just a few minutes old. I thought to myself, "I'll keep you warm tonight sweet baby. I will protect you, baby Jesus."

But that is not all. Not by a long shot. I was content to hold the baby in my arms all night long, realizing the precious responsibility I had to keep the child warm. But then I heard the voices of men. Even their whispers of excitement were loud as they approached the barn.

"Excuse us," said a man at the barn door. "I am Benjamin, a shepherd. My brothers, Matthew and Daniel, and I were taking care of our sheep tonight in the field not far from here. We were visited tonight by ….by….."

"By an angel," continued Matthew. "He appeared and told us not to be afraid because he was a messenger from God. He said that today, the Savior was born right here in Bethlehem. He said he was the Messiah, the Lord."

Benjamin added with great excitement, "And the angel said we would find the Savior as a baby, wrapped up in cloth and laying in a manger."

"Then the sky lit up like daytime," shared Daniel. "It looked like a thousand angels, all glowing with the light of God. And they said, 'Glory to God in the highest, and on earth good will to men.' Then like the snap of a finger, they were all gone."

Benjamin knelt on one knee and looked at Joseph, “May we please see the child born to you and your wife this night?”
Joseph looked at Mary, who nodded her head in agreement, and then said to the shepherds, “We cannot deny you what God has promised. Please come and see our son, Jesus.”
Oh, yes, the shepherds came and looked at the baby that I held in my arms. This baby Jesus was the long-awaited Messiah, the Savior, the Lord. This baby was sent from God and I, little Toothpick, was the one selected to be his first cradle.

It might have been my imagination, but it seemed like the inside of the barn glowed with a golden light of peace and joy. As I felt the baby move in my arms, I remembered my family. I was so proud of my father and my grandfather and my uncle. But then I realized how blessed I was to be the manger for the son of God. I thought I would feel proud of myself, but instead, I felt humbled, knowing that I did not deserve this blessing.

I did not think of the other trees in the forest, those big trees that put me down. I did not feel sad for being small. I was happy to be Toothpick, a little tree that was loved by a young boy and his calf. I was old and a little warped and in need of some fresh paint, and yet God chose to use me.

As the shepherds turned to leave, all I could think of was the voice of the angels, 'Glory to God in the highest, and on earth good will to men.' Only one word came to my mind, "Amen! Amen!"

THE
END

www.ingramcontent.com/pod-product-compliance
Lightning Source LLC
LaVergne TN
LVHW040923150826
845672LV00007B/2176